# LEADING *a* LIFE *of* INTEGRITY, EXCELLENCE, *and* RESULTS

*Business and Career Journal*

Paula

*published by*

BRONZE
BOW PUB.

All Scriptures are taken from the New King James Version. Copyright © 1982 by Thomas Nelson, Inc. Used by permission. All rights reserved.

ISBN 1-932458-41-7

Published by Bronze Bow Publishing, Inc. and Paula White Ministries.

Bronze Bow Publishing Inc.,
2600 E. 26th Street, Minneapolis, MN 55406

You can reach Bronze Bow Publishing on the Internet at www.bronzebowpublishing.com.

Paula White Ministries
P.O. Box 25151
Tampa, Florida 33622

You can reach Paula White Ministries on the Internet at www.paulawhite.org.

Literary development and cover/interior design by Koechel Peterson & Associates, Inc., Minneapolis, Minnesota.

Manufactured in Hong Kong

*"You are the salt of the earth....*
*You are the light of the world....*
*Let your light so shine before men,*
*that they may see your good works*
*and glorify your Father in heaven."*

MATTHEW 5:13–16

# INTRODUCTION

*Where do you go to get advice regarding your business and career?* There are many wonderful resources available to the savvy-minded business executives and "eager beavers" who are trying to scurry up the ladder of success. The latest *New York Times* best-seller on business or *Business Week* magazine or the *Wall Street Journal* are high on the list of must-reads for these driven individuals. Some seek out personal mentors, career coaches, role models in their career field, or a person with an impressive title behind his or her name. We look in many places, and they all have their place. But let's not forget the ultimate source on guidance for business and career—the Bible.

PERHAPS THE BIBLE IS SO OBVIOUS A SOURCE THAT WE SIMPLY OVERLOOK IT. Both the Old and New Testament are filled with illustrations of good business principles and rulers of great empires. The Book of Proverbs relates ethical principles, truths, and examples that relate to any workplace or career. Everyone faces challenges in their career—whether it's stress, frustration, dealing with customers and salespeople, and making sufficient income to pay all the bills. The Bible gives us clear instructions on how to deal with these obstacles as we go about our daily work.

Even as we deal with the politics and demands of business and career, Jesus commands us to be salt and light wherever we go. And sometimes that can be so difficult! Yet we are exhorted to be people of excellence as we walk in integrity. Our character is seen in the decisions we make, the priorities we develop, and the perspective we see issues through. It is foolish to think that the Enemy will not work overtime to weaken our integrity and cause us to be withdrawn in the workplace.

AND WHEN IT COMES TO OUR CAREER, IT IS CRITICAL THAT WE FIND BALANCE IN OUR LIVES. LIFE IS A RACE, AND WE MUST PACE OURSELVES. Almost everyone is faced with too much to do and not enough time, forcing them to juggle the demands of work and home. Most of us get caught up in the reigning culture of success that demands an intensity of devotion that is unhealthy and destructive. It is all too easy to slip into the pattern of giving our career and business the time and attention that we should be giving to God, our families, and ourselves. Through living an unbalanced life, it is possible for any of us to come to the end of our careers as King David did—incredibly successful by the world's standards, but alone with family heartaches and failures that would break anyone's heart. Overloaded people fail—that's the true bottom line.

In this journal, I hope that you'll take the opportunity to consider your business and career life in the light of God's Word. What discoveries are you making about your life? Are you being salt and light? Are you keeping your priorities balanced? WHAT IS GOD CHALLENGING YOU TO DO? YOUR DAILY THOUGHTS WILL TELL THE STORY.

# WHY JOURNAL?

IF YOU HAVE EVER DOUBTED THE IMPORTANCE AND
VALUE OF KEEPING A JOURNAL, YOU NEED LOOK NO
FURTHER THAN THE NEW TESTAMENT. The books of
Matthew, Mark, Luke, and John are the accounts of four men who
took the time to record the events of their day as they walked with
Jesus. Their writings provide a manuscript through which we can
know the ways of God, hear His voice, and put into practice the
teachings of Christ.

Your walk with God and your relationship and commitment to your
career deserves the same attention. I want you to freely express your
thoughts on any area of your business and career life that God shines
His light upon—whether it is your personal integrity and witness, your
spiritual life, your relationship with your spouse and children, your
finances, your hobbies, your friendships, your commitment to your
church, or whatever. It is important that you express the honest
answers of your heart. If you find imbalance, don't try to hide or
excuse it. If God exposes any lack of integrity, He will transform you

with His truth. Listen to God and read His Word to discover what
it is that He desires from you. Whenever God speaks, His message is
always worth recording.

Journaling is an exercise that has enhanced my faith walk and has
revealed God's faithfulness in my life as I have learned to trust Him.
It has created a lasting record of my conversations with God. In the
stillness and sanctity of my journal time, God's voice is loudest in my
life. It's through my volumes and volumes of journals that I have found
a lasting record of my friendship with God.

I wish the very same for you.

*Paula*

# How to Use This Journal

I'VE ALWAYS KEPT A JOURNAL, AND I HAVE CHERISHED THE PRIVILEGE OF SPEAKING DIRECTLY TO GOD THROUGH PRAYER SINCE THE DAY I PUT MY FAITH IN JESUS CHRIST. So prayer journaling, in particular, came quite naturally to me. What I didn't know early on was that I would actually be able to have conversations with God, to talk to and hear back from Him. The beautiful poetic language of the King James Bible intimidated me. I thought I had to speak to God in the language of Abraham or David. Not so.

When you speak to God, it does not have to be formal. James 2:23 says that because Abraham believed in God, he was a friend of God. Do you believe in God? Well, then you, too, are His friend. Formalities such as *thee* and *thou* can be put aside for casual terms of endearment such as *Daddy* and *Father*. He just wants to hear from you. Speak to Him from your heart, and He will speak to you from His.

Dedicating a "journal time" each day will help you to get into the routine of journaling. Choose a quiet, private place to shut out the cares of the world and steal away with God. Perhaps a good time for you is just before retiring for the evening or in the morning before the rest of your family awakes. It may help to play soothing worship music to calm your mind and quiet the distractions of the day.

Be sure to notate the date at the beginning of each entry. This will be particularly interesting to you as you reflect back over the pages later on. Then check the box that best describes your journal entry for the day. Are you expressing what you are discovering about your business and career life? Are you recording what you believe God is challenging you to do—perhaps to make a change of priorities or to take a stand for truth where you might have previously drawn back? Take as much space as you need to jot down whatever you feel or are thinking, running into several pages if necessary. Allow yourself to flow freely, releasing any tensions, anxieties, or worries to God through your pen. Talk to Him, listen to Him, commune with Him. The more often you do it, the more natural it will feel.

Habakkuk 2:2 encourages us to "write the vision and make it plain on tablets, that he may run who reads it." Periodically throughout this journal, you will find "Reflections" pages. These pages are intended to give you an opportunity to review several entries at a time so that you can see your own personal growth and to remind you of the desires you have written. They also provide you the opportunity to reflect on all that God has spoken to you and performed in your life. Take every opportunity to appreciate the smallest answered prayer and to meditate on God's faithfulness.

HEAVENLY FATHER, REVEAL YOURSELF TO ME THIS DAY. BRING FORTH WISDOM AND REVELATION KNOWLEDGE AS YOU TEACH ME, BY MAKING YOUR WAY KNOWN. TEACH ME HOW TO BE CONFORMED TO THE IMAGE OF JESUS CHRIST, SO THAT I CAN WALK IN COMPLETE OBEDIENCE TO YOUR WORD AND PRAY WITHOUT CEASING.

☐ *Today's challenges and triumphs . . .*

☐ *God is helping me to . . .*

"You did not choose Me,
but I chose you and appointed you
that you should go and bear fruit,
and that your fruit should remain,
that whatever you ask the Father
in My name He may give you."

JOHN 15:16

☐ *Today's challenges and triumphs . . .*

☐ *God is helping me to . . .*

What you believe about yourself
virtually dictates how successful
you are in every area of your life.

☐ *Today's challenges and triumphs . . .*

☐ *God is helping me to . . .*

It's not what we

see in the mirror

that defines

who we are.

We are not

defined by what

we have but

who we are.

☐ *Today's challenges and triumphs . . .*

☐ *God is helping me to . . .*

*As a man thinketh
in his heart, so is he.*

PROVERBS 4:23 KJV

☐ *Today's challenges and triumphs . . .*

☐ *God is helping me to . . .*

You have been engineered
by God to be a success.

☐ *Today's challenges and triumphs . . .*

☐ *God is helping me to . . .*

Quit comparing

yourself to every-

one around you

and copying what

they're doing.

You are the

Designer's

original.

☐ *Today's challenges and triumphs . . .*

☐ *God is helping me to . . .*

*And let the beauty of the LORD our God be upon us, and establish the work of our hands for us; yes, establish the work of our hands.*

PSALM 90:17

☐ *Today's challenges and triumphs . . .*

☐ *God is helping me to . . .*

THE QUESTION IS NOT HOW LONG WE

LIVE BUT HOW WELL WE LIVE. WHAT MATTERS ARE

THE MOMENTS WE LIVE LIFE TO THE FULLEST.

☐ *Today's challenges and triumphs . . .*

☐ *God is helping me to . . .*

The challenges handed to you
in life are trying to push you
into your destiny.

☐ Today's challenges and triumphs . . .

☐ God is helping me to . . .

"This Book of the Law shall not depart from your mouth, but
you shall meditate in it day and night, that you may observe to
do according to all that is written in it.
For then you will make your way prosperous, and then you will
have good success. Have I not commanded you?
Be strong and of good courage; do not be afraid, nor be
dismayed, for the LORD your God is with you wherever you go."

JOSHUA 1:8–9

☐ *Today's challenges and triumphs . . .*
☐ *God is helping me to . . .*

My home

Your future is
determined by the
decisions you make,
the priorities you
develop, and the
perspective you see
things through.

☐ *Today's challenges and triumphs . . .*

☐ *God is helping me to . . .*

*If you can see the invisible,
you can do the impossible.*

☐ *Today's challenges and triumphs . . .*

☐ *God is helping me to . . .*

*The LORD is on my side; I will not fear. What can man do to me? It is better to trust in the LORD than to put confidence in man. It is better to trust in the LORD than to put confidence in princes.*

PSALM 118:6, 8–9

□ *Today's challenges and triumphs . . .*

□ *God is helping me to . . .*

Don't let life falsely label
you. God will make you
"larger than life."

☐ *Today's challenges and triumphs . . .*

☐ *God is helping me to . . .*

YOU MUST "THINK BIG" TO DO
GOD-SIZED THINGS. NOTHING BIG EVER
COMES FROM THINKING SMALL.

☐ *Today's challenges and triumphs . . .*

☐ *God is helping me to . . .*

*And whatever you do in word or deed, do all in the name of the Lord Jesus, giving thanks to God the Father through Him.*

COLOSSIANS 3:17

☐ *Today's challenges and triumphs . . .*

☐ *God is helping me to . . .*

Every day God

affords you the

opportunity to

make your mark,

impact your world,

and take yourself

to the next level.

☐ *Today's challenges and triumphs . . .*

☐ *God is helping me to . . .*

> There is power working
> inwardly that is much
> greater than anything
> exteriorly.

☐ *Today's challenges and triumphs . . .*

☐ *God is helping me to . . .*

*Every word of God is pure;*
*He is a shield to those who*
*put their trust in Him.*

PROVERBS 30:5

☐ *Today's challenges and triumphs . . .*

☐ *God is helping me to . . .*

...........................................................................................................................

...........................................................................................................................

...........................................................................................................................

...........................................................................................................................

...........................................................................................................................

...........................................................................................................................

...........................................................................................................................

Stop living by what you feel
and live by what God says.

...........................................................................................................................

...........................................................................................................................

...........................................................................................................................

...........................................................................................................................

...........................................................................................................................

...........................................................................................................................

...........................................................................................................................

...........................................................................................................................

...........................................................................................................................

...........................................................................................................................

...........................................................................................................................

☐ *Today's challenges and triumphs . . .*
☐ *God is helping me to . . .*

A person with a
past can touch a
God in the present
who is able to
change the future.

☐ *Today's challenges and triumphs . . .*

☐ *God is helping me to . . .*

*Now to Him who is able to do exceedingly
abundantly above all that we ask or think,
according to the power that works in us,
to Him be glory in the church by Christ Jesus
to all generations, forever and ever. Amen.*

EPHESIANS 3:20–21

☐ *Today's challenges and triumphs . . .*

☐ *God is helping me to . . .*

Build a dream

beyond your means.

Life is too short

to think small.

☐ *Today's challenges and triumphs . . .*
☐ *God is helping me to . . .*

God is not intimidated by your
aspirations. He gave them to you,
so go for it.

☐ *Today's challenges and triumphs . . .*
☐ *God is helping me to . . .*

*For I know the thoughts that I think toward you,
says the LORD, thoughts of peace and not of evil,
to give you a future and a hope. Then you will call
upon Me and go and pray to Me, and I will listen
to you. And you will seek Me and find Me, when
you search for Me with all your heart.*

JEREMIAH 29:11–13

☐ *Today's challenges and triumphs . . .*

☐ *God is helping me to . . .*

It is scientifically proven that the bumblebee cannot fly—his wingspan is too short for his body weight—but nobody ever told the bumblebee.

☐ *Today's challenges and triumphs . . .*

☐ *God is helping me to . . .*

Don't despise small beginnings—
they can turn into large endings.

☐ *Today's challenges and triumphs . . .*
☐ *God is helping me to . . .*

*"For with God nothing will
be impossible."*

LUKE 1:37

☐ *Today's challenges and triumphs . . .*

☐ *God is helping me to . . .*

LITTLE PEOPLE CAN DO BIG THINGS.
YOUR ATTITUDE DETERMINES
YOUR ALTITUDE.

☐ *Today's challenges and triumphs . . .*
☐ *God is helping me to . . .*

God will always give you another
chance: the choice is yours to
take it. Choice, not chance,
determines destiny.

☐ *Today's challenges and triumphs . . .*

☐ *God is helping me to . . .*

Expectancy is the breeding

ground for miracles.

☐ *Today's challenges and triumphs . . .*
☐ *God is helping me to . . .*

_____

_____

_____

_____

_____

_____

_____

_____

_____

_____

_____

*But now, thus says the LORD, who created you,*
*O Jacob, and He who formed you, O Israel:*
*"Fear not, for I have redeemed you; I have called you*
*by your name; you are Mine. When you pass*
*through the waters, I will be with you;*
*and through the rivers, they shall not overflow you.*
*When you walk through the fire, you shall not be*
*burned, nor shall the flame scorch you."*

ISAIAH 43:1–2

☐ *Today's challenges and triumphs . . .*

☐ *God is helping me to . . .*

Passionate people
find the power to
push through
every obstacle
holding them
back.

☐ *Today's challenges and triumphs . . .*

☐ *God is helping me to . . .*

You might be disappointed
if you fail, but you are
doomed if you never try.

☐ *Today's challenges and triumphs . . .*

☐ *God is helping me to . . .*

Failure is not falling down but staying down. Do not fear mistakes— fail your way to success.

☐ *Today's challenges and triumphs . . .*

☐ *God is helping me to . . .*

........................................................................................................

........................................................................................................

........................................................................................................

........................................................................................................

........................................................................................................

........................................................................................................

........................................................................................................

........................................................................................................

........................................................................................................

........................................................................................................

........................................................................................................

........................................................................................................

........................................................................................................

........................................................................................................

........................................................................................................

*"You whom I have taken from the ends of the earth,*
*and called from its farthest regions, and said to you,*
*You are My servant, I have chosen you and have not cast you away:*
*fear not, for I am with you; be not dismayed, for I am your God.*
*I will strengthen you, yes, I will help you, I will uphold you*
*with My righteous right hand."*

ISAIAH 41:9–10

☐ *Today's challenges and triumphs . . .*

☐ *God is helping me to . . .*

Opening the door to your future requires shutting the door to your past. You cannot look ahead and look behind you at the same time. There is no future in the past.

☐ *Today's challenges and triumphs . . .*

☐ *God is helping me to . . .*

*But one thing I do, forgetting those
things which are behind and reaching for-
ward to those things which are ahead,
I press toward the goal for the prize of the
upward call of God in Christ Jesus.*

PHILIPPIANS 3:13–14

☐ *Today's challenges and triumphs . . .*
☐ *God is helping me to . . .*

No one wakes up
polished.
You must be
developed.
To endure means
to stand firm
under pressure.

☐ *Today's challenges and triumphs . . .*

☐ *God is helping me to . . .*

For every blessing there is
testing. For every opportunity
there is adversity. Trouble is an
incubator for greatness.

☐ *Today's challenges and triumphs . . .*

☐ *God is helping me to . . .*

*My brethren, count it all joy when you fall into various trials, knowing that the testing of your faith produces patience. But let patience have its perfect work, that you may be perfect and complete, lacking nothing.*

JAMES 1:2–4

☐ *Today's challenges and triumphs . . .*

☐ *God is helping me to . . .*

THE DOOR OF OPPORTUNITY SWINGS ON THE HINGES OF OPPOSITION. YOU DON'T CONQUER WITHOUT CONFLICT. YOU DON'T WIN WITHOUT WAR.

# Reflections 1

When Joseph was sold into slavery in Egypt, he could have become bitter and angry. Instead, he chose to humbly serve God . . . and became phenomenally successful: "The LORD was with Joseph, and he was a successful man; and he was in the house of his master the Egyptian. And his master saw that the LORD was with him and that the LORD made all he did to prosper in his hand" (Genesis 39:2–3). If God can do this in Joseph's situation, He can do it in yours as well.

Take time to review the last several pages of this journal. Reflect on all the things you have been discovering about your life. As you've thought about your life in the light of God's Word, what are you learning? What are the most important desires you are expressing to God? What are you discovering that God desires from you? How is He working in your life?

## Capture your thoughts below.

..........................................................................................

..........................................................................................

..........................................................................................

..........................................................................................

☐ *Today's challenges and triumphs . . .*

☐ *God is helping me to . . .*

The big four confidence destroyers
the devil uses are: anxiety,
depression, guilt, and anger.

□ *Today's challenges and triumphs . . .*
□ *God is helping me to . . .*

As long as you
don't quit, you will
never lose.
Never give up
on yourself.

☐ *Today's challenges and triumphs . . .*

☐ *God is helping me to . . .*

☐ *Today's challenges and triumphs . . .*

☐ *God is helping me to . . .*

Successful people do daily what
others do occasionally. Promotion
comes as a result of faithfulness.

☐ *Today's challenges and triumphs . . .*

☐ *God is helping me to . . .*

_"Hear, O Israel: Today you are on the verge of battle with your enemies. Do not let your heart faint, do not be afraid, and do not tremble or be terrified because of them; for the LORD your God is He who goes with you, to fight for you against your enemies, to save you."_

DEUTERONOMY 20:3–4

☐ *Today's challenges and triumphs . . .*
☐ *God is helping me to . . .*

My home

If you really want

to do something,

you will find a way.

For any new level

in life, there is a

"cost of admission"—

pay the price.

☐ *Today's challenges and triumphs . . .*

☐ *God is helping me to . . .*

*The plans of the diligent lead surely to plenty, but those of everyone who is hasty, surely to poverty.*

PROVERBS 21:5

☐ *Today's challenges and triumphs . . .*

☐ *God is helping me to . . .*

Be flexible. You will need to bend
in life. Attitude is a little thing
that makes a big difference.

☐ *Today's challenges and triumphs . . .*

☐ *God is helping me to . . .*

Motivation is deeper than words.
Motives have a lot to do with
who you are.

☐ *Today's challenges and triumphs . . .*

☐ *God is helping me to . . .*

*I can do all things through Christ who strengthens me.... And my God shall supply all your need according to His riches in glory by Christ Jesus.*

PHILIPPIANS 4:13, 19

☐ *Today's challenges and triumphs . . .*
☐ *God is helping me to . . .*

People either add,
subtract, multiply,
or divide in your
life. "Do not be
deceived: 'Evil
company corrupts
good habits'"
(1 Corinthians 15:33).

☐ *Today's challenges and triumphs . . .*

☐ *God is helping me to . . .*

Recognize that those who reject you

have no ability to see inside you.

Find people who enhance you

rather than inhibit you.

☐ *Today's challenges and triumphs . . .*

☐ *God is helping me to . . .*

*For God has not given us a
spirit of fear, but of power and of
love and of a sound mind.*

2 TIMOTHY 1:7

☐ *Today's challenges and triumphs . . .*

☐ *God is helping me to . . .*

You cannot control circumstances,
but you can control your
response.

□ *Today's challenges and triumphs . . .*
□ *God is helping me to . . .*

To have anxiety is to worry about something that has not happened and may never occur.

☐ *Today's challenges and triumphs . . .*

☐ *God is helping me to . . .*

*Be anxious for nothing, but in everything by prayer and suppli-
cation, with thanksgiving, let your requests be made known to
God; and the peace of God, which surpasses all understanding,
will guard your hearts and minds through Christ Jesus.*

PHILIPPIANS 4:6–7

☐ *Today's challenges and triumphs . . .*

☐ *God is helping me to . . .*

Self-confidence leads to achievement. Stop waiting on someone
to acknowledge your gifting to
validate you.

☐ *Today's challenges and triumphs . . .*

☐ *God is helping me to . . .*

Don't spend a

lifetime trying to be

what you were not

created to be.

Be authentically you.

☐ *Today's challenges and triumphs . . .*

☐ *God is helping me to . . .*

*By the grace of God I am
what I am, and His grace
toward me was not in vain.*

1 CORINTHIANS 15:10

☐ *Today's challenges and triumphs . . .*
☐ *God is helping me to . . .*

When God calls
you, He equips you.
It's time to discover
new strengths
within yourself
and build on them
to achieve your
God-given potential
and goals.

☐ *Today's challenges and triumphs . . .*

☐ *God is helping me to . . .*

DISCOVER YOUR PASSION, AND THEN
FIND A WAY TO MAKE MONEY WITH IT.
IF PEOPLE DON'T KNOW WHAT YOUR
PASSION IS, YOU DON'T HAVE ONE.

☐ *Today's challenges and triumphs . . .*

☐ *God is helping me to . . .*

*Now may the God of peace who brought up our Lord Jesus from the dead, that great Shepherd of the sheep, through the blood of the everlasting covenant, make you complete in every good work to do His will, working in you what is well pleasing in His sight, through Jesus Christ, to whom be glory forever and ever. Amen.*

HEBREWS 13:20–21

☐ *Today's challenges and triumphs . . .*

☐ *God is helping me to . . .*

If you don't know where you are
going, you are already there. If you
fail to plan, you plan to fail.

☐ *Today's challenges and triumphs . . .*

☐ *God is helping me to . . .*

Go confidently in the direction
of your dreams. Live the life
you imagined.

☐ *Today's challenges and triumphs . . .*

☐ *God is helping me to . . .*

*I will instruct you and
teach you in the way you
should go; I will guide you
with My eye.*

PSALM 32:8

☐ *Today's challenges and triumphs . . .*

☐ *God is helping me to . . .*

You frame your world by the
words you speak. If you want
to know how you think, listen
to your mouth.

☐ *Today's challenges and triumphs . . .*

☐ *God is helping me to . . .*

Complaining causes
you to remain.
Praising causes you
to be raised.

☐ *Today's challenges and triumphs . . .*

☐ *God is helping me to . . .*

*Death and life are in the power of
the tongue, and those who love it
will eat its fruit.*

PROVERBS 18:21

☐ *Today's challenges and triumphs . . .*

☐ *God is helping me to . . .*

Blessing is not just money—it is the empowerment to prosper and succeed. Never allow money to control your mission.

☐ *Today's challenges and triumphs . . .*

☐ *God is helping me to . . .*

Your checkbook is a book of revelation. It reveals where your heart is.

☐ *Today's challenges and triumphs . . .*

☐ *God is helping me to . . .*

*"For where your treasure is, there your heart will be also....
No one can serve two masters; for either he will hate the one
and love the other, or else he will be loyal to the one and despise
the other. You cannot serve God and mammon."*

MATTHEW 6:21, 24

☐ *Today's challenges and triumphs . . .*

☐ *God is helping me to . . .*

Map your success.
Approach each step
as a separate
mission, and you
will eventually
arrive at the end
of the goal.

☐ *Today's challenges and triumphs . . .*

☐ *God is helping me to . . .*

If opportunity doesn't knock,
then build a door. Initiate your
blessing. Nothing significant will
happen until you initiate it.

☐ *Today's challenges and triumphs . . .*

☐ *God is helping me to . . .*

*"Bring all the tithes into the storehouse, that there may be food in My house, and try Me now in this," says the LORD of hosts, "if I will not open for you the windows of heaven and pour out for you such blessing that there will not be room enough to receive it."*

MALACHI 3:10

☐ *Today's challenges and triumphs . . .*

☐ *God is helping me to . . .*

God will only

promote you as

high as your

character will take

you. You cannot go

beyond limitations

of your character.

☐ *Today's challenges and triumphs . . .*

☐ *God is helping me to . . .*

Right is right if
no one is doing it,
and wrong is wrong
if everyone is doing
it. To be disciplined
means to do the
right thing when you
feel like doing the
wrong thing.

☐ *Today's challenges and triumphs . . .*

☐ *God is helping me to . . .*

*"He who is faithful in what is least is faithful also in much;
and he who is unjust in what is least is unjust also in much.
Therefore if you have not been faithful in the unrighteous
mammon, who will commit to your trust the true riches?
And if you have not been faithful in what is another man's,
who will give you what is your own?"*

LUKE 16:10–12

☐ *Today's challenges and triumphs . . .*

☐ *God is helping me to . . .*

ALL ACHIEVEMENT AND ALL EARTHLY

RICHES HAVE THEIR BEGINNINGS IN AN

IDEA OR DREAM.

☐ *Today's challenges and triumphs . . .*

☐ *God is helping me to . . .*

Desire is the birthplace of
productivity and fulfillment.
There can be no fulfillment
where there is no passion.

☐ *Today's challenges and triumphs . . .*

☐ *God is helping me to . . .*

*"Why do you spend money for what is not bread,
and your wages for what does not satisfy?
Listen carefully to Me, and eat what is good,
and let your soul delight itself in abundance.
Incline your ear, and come to Me. Hear, and your
soul shall live; and I will make an everlasting
covenant with you—the sure mercies of David."*

ISAIAH 55:2–3

☐ *Today's challenges and triumphs . . .*

☐ *God is helping me to . . .*

HE WHO IS GOOD AT
MAKING EXCUSES IS
SELDOM GOOD AT ANYTHING ELSE.

☐ *Today's challenges and triumphs . . .*

☐ *God is helping me to . . .*

☐ *Today's challenges and triumphs . . .*

☐ *God is helping me to . . .*

When you always use an excuse,

you give up the power to change.

☐ *Today's challenges and triumphs . . .*
☐ *God is helping me to . . .*

*"A good man out of the good treasure of his heart brings
forth good; and an evil man out of the evil treasure of his heart
brings forth evil. For out of the abundance of the heart
his mouth speaks."*

LUKE 6:45

☐ *Today's challenges and triumphs . . .*

☐ *God is helping me to . . .*

God will cause the
wall in your life to
fall down, and your
barrier will become
your bridge.

# Reflections 2

Consider your career in the light of these words: "For the eyes of the LORD run to and fro throughout the whole earth, to show Himself strong on behalf of those whose heart is loyal to Him" (2 Chronicles 16:9). I hope you catch a sense of how excited that God is to bless you and work in your life as you commit yourself completely to Him!

Take time to review the last several pages of this journal. Reflect on all the things you have been discovering about your life. As you've thought about your life in the light of God's Word, what are you learning? What are the most important desires you are expressing to God? What are you discovering that God desires from you? How is He working in your life?

## Capture your thoughts below.

☐ *Today's challenges and triumphs* . . .

☐ *God is helping me to* . . .

Mountains don't move unless you

speak to them.

☐ *Today's challenges and triumphs . . .*

☐ *God is helping me to . . .*

*So Jesus answered and said to them, "Assuredly, I say to you, if you have faith and do not doubt, you will not only do what was done to the fig tree, but also if you say to this mountain, 'Be removed and be cast into the sea,' it will be done."*

MATTHEW 21:21

☐ *Today's challenges and triumphs . . .*

☐ *God is helping me to . . .*

When you write down a goal,
you increase the percentage of
achieving it 90 times.

☐ *Today's challenges and triumphs . . .*

☐ *God is helping me to . . .*

Set goals that make

you rely on God.

☐ *Today's challenges and triumphs . . .*

☐ *God is helping me to . . .*

*Jesus said to her, "Did I not say to you that if you would believe you would see the glory of God?"*

JOHN 11:40

☐ *Today's challenges and triumphs . . .*

☐ *God is helping me to . . .*

Only those who risk going too far

will ever know how far they can go.

☐ *Today's challenges and triumphs . . .*
☐ *God is helping me to . . .*

You will never know what's in you
if you dwell in the darkness of
yesterday.

☐ *Today's challenges and triumphs . . .*

☐ *God is helping me to . . .*

*Let them shout for joy and be glad, who favor my righteous
cause; and let them say continually, "Let the LORD be magnified,
who has pleasure in the prosperity of His servant."*

PSALM 35:27

☐ *Today's challenges and triumphs . . .*

☐ *God is helping me to . . .*

EVERYTHING YOU NEED IN LIFE IS WITHIN. DISCOVER YOUR RESOURCES AND DEVELOP THEM.

☐ *Today's challenges and triumphs . . .*

☐ *God is helping me to . . .*

*Being confident of this very thing, that He who has begun a good work in you will complete it until the day of Jesus Christ.*

PHILIPPIANS 1:6–7

☐ *Today's challenges and triumphs . . .*

☐ *God is helping me to . . .*

The person who never changes his opinion never corrects his mistakes.

☐ *Today's challenges and triumphs . . .*

☐ *God is helping me to . . .*

Stability is a sign of maturity.

☐ *Today's challenges and triumphs . . .*

☐ *God is helping me to . . .*

*Therefore, my beloved brethren, be
steadfast, immovable, always abounding
in the work of the Lord, knowing that
your labor is not in vain in the Lord.*

1 CORINTHIANS 15:58

☐ *Today's challenges and triumphs . . .*

☐ *God is helping me to . . .*

Your imagination needs
stimulation of association with
significant others.

☐ *Today's challenges and triumphs . . .*

☐ *God is helping me to . . .*

Anyone can be more

creative. It starts

by looking for

new solutions . . .

by not being

satisfied with the

first answer you

come up with.

☐ *Today's challenges and triumphs . . .*
☐ *God is helping me to . . .*

☐ *Today's challenges and triumphs . . .*

☐ *God is helping me to . . .*

*The LORD will guide you continually,
and satisfy your soul in drought,
and strengthen your bones; you shall be
like a watered garden, and like a spring of
water, whose waters do not fail.*

ISAIAH 58:11

☐ *Today's challenges and triumphs . . .*

☐ *God is helping me to . . .*

A leader does not imitate

but rather creates.

☐ *Today's challenges and triumphs . . .*

☐ *God is helping me to . . .*

Mentors are your gate to greatness
and your bridge to blessings.

☐ *Today's challenges and triumphs . . .*

☐ *God is helping me to . . .*

*For by wise counsel you will wage
your own war, and in a multitude
of counselors there is safety.*

PROVERBS 24:6

☐ *Today's challenges and triumphs . . .*

☐ *God is helping me to . . .*

Your greatest weaknesses will stop

your greatest desires.

☐ *Today's challenges and triumphs . . .*

☐ *God is helping me to . . .*

You can have excellence
without arrogance.

☐ Today's challenges and triumphs . . .

☐ God is helping me to . . .

Now the man Moses was very
humble, more than all men who
were on the face of the earth.

NUMBERS 12:3

☐ *Today's challenges and triumphs . . .*

☐ *God is helping me to . . .*

Defining moments are how you

got to be the person that you are.

☐ *Today's challenges and triumphs . . .*
☐ *God is helping me to . . .*

No one becomes successful
by accident.

☐ *Today's challenges and triumphs . . .*
☐ *God is helping me to . . .*

*Do not be deceived, God is not
mocked; for whatever a man
sows, that he will also reap.*

GALATIANS 6:7

☐ *Today's challenges and triumphs . . .*

☐ *God is helping me to . . .*

Some of the
people who fight
you are preparing
you for where
you're going.

☐ *Today's challenges and triumphs . . .*
☐ *God is helping me to . . .*

*"But those who wait on the LORD shall renew their strength;
they shall mount up with wings like eagles, they shall run
and not be weary, they shall walk and not faint."*

ISAIAH 40:31

☐ *Today's challenges and triumphs . . .*

☐ *God is helping me to . . .*

Don't let your history hinder you
from your destiny.

☐ *Today's challenges and triumphs . . .*

☐ *God is helping me to . . .*

"SUCCESS" ONLY COMES BEFORE
"WORK" IN THE DICTIONARY.

☐ *Today's challenges and triumphs . . .*

☐ *God is helping me to . . .*

If you always please man,
you will displease God.

......................................................................................................

......................................................................................................

......................................................................................................

......................................................................................................

......................................................................................................

......................................................................................................

......................................................................................................

......................................................................................................

......................................................................................................

......................................................................................................

......................................................................................................

......................................................................................................

......................................................................................................

......................................................................................................

......................................................................................................

......................................................................................................

☐ *Today's challenges and triumphs . . .*

☐ *God is helping me to . . .*

*For do I now persuade men, or
God? Or do I seek to please men?
For if I still pleased men, I would
not be a bondservant of Christ.*

GALATIANS 1:10

☐ *Today's challenges and triumphs . . .*

☐ *God is helping me to . . .*

People don't follow titles.

They follow courage.

☐ *Today's challenges and triumphs . . .*

☐ *God is helping me to . . .*

You will influence
others only to the
portion you are
willing to sacrifice
yourself.

☐ *Today's challenges and triumphs . . .*
☐ *God is helping me to . . .*

*"Whoever desires to become great among you, let him be your servant. And whoever desires to be first among you, let him be your slave."*

MATTHEW 20:26–27

☐ *Today's challenges and triumphs . . .*
☐ *God is helping me to . . .*

Give people what
they need to get
started—a goal
and a timetable—
and you have a
good chance at
obtaining your
objective.

☐ *Today's challenges and triumphs . . .*

☐ *God is helping me to . . .*

When bringing correction,

use the sandwich technique:

(+) positive / (-) negative / (+) positive.

☐ *Today's challenges and triumphs . . .*

☐ *God is helping me to . . .*

*Let your speech always be with grace, seasoned with salt, that you may know how you ought to answer each one.*

COLOSSIANS 4:6

☐ *Today's challenges and triumphs . . .*

☐ *God is helping me to . . .*

ONE OF YOUR GREATEST GIFTS
IS THE ABILITY TO SEE BEYOND
WHERE YOU ARE RIGHT NOW.

☐ *Today's challenges and triumphs . . .*

☐ *God is helping me to . . .*

If you don't know where you are

going, you are already there.

☐ *Today's challenges and triumphs . . .*

☐ *God is helping me to . . .*

*He sought God in the days of Zechariah, who had understanding
in the visions of God; and as long as he sought the LORD,
God made him prosper.*

2 CHRONICLES 26:5

# *Reflections* 3

Daniel was taken as a captive from Jerusalem to the foreign city of Babylon, where his character and commitment to God caused him to not only survive but to rise to highest levels of success. Not only did King Nebuchadnezzar acknowledge to Daniel, "Truly your God is the God of gods, the LORD of kings, and a revealer of secrets," but he made Daniel ruler over the whole province of Babylon, and chief administrator over all the wise men of Babylon (Daniel 2:46–48).

Take time to review the last several pages of this journal. Reflect on all the things you have been discovering about your life. As you've thought about your life in the light of God's Word, what are you learning? What are the most important desires you are expressing to God? What are you discovering that God desires from you? How is He working in your life?

## Capture your thoughts below.

☐ *Today's challenges and triumphs . . .*

☐ *God is helping me to . . .*

Work hard

and play hard.

☐ *Today's challenges and triumphs . . .*

☐ *God is helping me to . . .*

*Nothing is better for a man than that he should eat and drink, and that his soul should enjoy good in his labor. This also, I saw, was from the hand of God.*

ECCLESIASTES 2:24

☐ *Today's challenges and triumphs . . .*

☐ *God is helping me to . . .*

When you need
something from
the outside to fix
something on the
inside, it's either
an addiction
or idolatry.

☐ *Today's challenges and triumphs . . .*

☐ *God is helping me to . . .*

For every person there will be a
problem, but for every problem
God has a prescription.

☐ *Today's challenges and triumphs . . .*

☐ *God is helping me to . . .*

*"Only take heed to yourself, and diligently keep yourself, lest you forget the things your eyes have seen, and lest they depart from your heart all the days of your life."*

DEUTERONOMY 4:9

☐ *Today's challenges and triumphs . . .*

☐ *God is helping me to . . .*

What you had for a long time can

depart from you in a short time.

☐ *Today's challenges and triumphs . . .*

☐ *God is helping me to . . .*

The building is only as tall as the foundation is strong enough to build on.

☐ *Today's challenges and triumphs . . .*

☐ *God is helping me to . . .*

*Better to be of a humble spirit
with the lowly, than to divide
the spoil with the proud.*

PROVERBS 16:19

□ *Today's challenges and triumphs . . .*
□ *God is helping me to . . .*

Choose your battles!

☐ *Today's challenges and triumphs . . .*

☐ *God is helping me to . . .*

You can disagree agreeably.

☐ *Today's challenges and triumphs . . .*

☐ *God is helping me to . . .*

☐ *Today's challenges and triumphs . . .*

☐ *God is helping me to . . .*

*He who is slow to anger is better
than the mighty, and he who rules
his spirit than he who takes a city.*

PROVERBS 16:32

☐ *Today's challenges and triumphs . . .*

☐ *God is helping me to . . .*

Don't go where the path may
lead. Make a path for yourself.

☐ *Today's challenges and triumphs . . .*

☐ *God is helping me to . . .*

*But the path of the just is like the shining sun,
that shines ever brighter unto the perfect day.*

PROVERBS 4:18

☐ *Today's challenges and triumphs . . .*

☐ *God is helping me to . . .*

Behavior permitted is behavior
accepted. Never complain about
what you tolerate.

☐ *Today's challenges and triumphs . . .*

☐ *God is helping me to . . .*

Behavior rewarded

is behavior repeated.

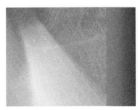

☐ *Today's challenges and triumphs . . .*

☐ *God is helping me to . . .*

Some of the
people who fight
you are preparing
you for where
you're going.

☐ *Today's challenges and triumphs . . .*

☐ *God is helping me to . . .*

*"Therefore, whatever you want men
to do to you, do also to them, for
this is the Law and the Prophets."*

MATTHEW 7:12

☐ *Today's challenges and triumphs . . .*

☐ *God is helping me to . . .*

INFORMATION IS POWER.
NEVER MAKE A DECISION
WITH LIMITED INFORMATION.

☐ *Today's challenges and triumphs . . .*

☐ *God is helping me to . . .*

Don't make a

judgment where

you have no

compassion.

☐ *Today's challenges and triumphs . . .*

☐ *God is helping me to . . .*

*He who answers a matter before he hears it, it is folly and shame to him.*

PROVERBS 18:13

☐ *Today's challenges and triumphs . . .*
☐ *God is helping me to . . .*

If you are empty, you have nothing to give. You give what you have.

☐ *Today's challenges and triumphs . . .*

☐ *God is helping me to . . .*

The person who never changes his
opinion never corrects his mistakes.

☐ *Today's challenges and triumphs . . .*

☐ *God is helping me to . . .*

Overloaded people fail.

☐ *Today's challenges and triumphs . . .*

☐ *God is helping me to . . .*

*Six days you shall do your work, and on the seventh day you shall rest, that your ox and your donkey may rest, and the son of your female servant and the stranger may be refreshed.*

EXODUS 23:12

☐ *Today's challenges and triumphs . . .*

☐ *God is helping me to . . .*

*What then shall we say to these things?*
*If God is for us, who can be against us?*
*He who did not spare His own Son,*
*but delivered Him up for us all,*
*how shall He not with Him also*
*freely give us all things?*

ROMANS 8:31–32

☐ *Today's challenges and triumphs . . .*

☐ *God is helping me to . . .*

If you are going
to play, then
play to win.

☐ *Today's challenges and triumphs . . .*

☐ *God is helping me to . . .*

History makers and world changers

are mere men and women.

☐ *Today's challenges and triumphs . . .*
☐ *God is helping me to . . .*

*Do you see a man who excels in his
work? He will stand before kings;
he will not stand before unknown men.*

PROVERBS 22:29

☐ *Today's challenges and triumphs . . .*

☐ *God is helping me to . . .*

A little job done is better than
a big job talked about.

☐ *Today's challenges and triumphs . . .*

☐ *God is helping me to . . .*

IT'S BETTER TO MOVE IN FAITH
THAN TO SIT IN DOUBT. FAITH IS WHAT
MOVES GOD.

☐ *Today's challenges and triumphs . . .*

☐ *God is helping me to . . .*

You can't conquer

what you don't

confront. You

can't confront

what you don't

identify.

☐ *Today's challenges and triumphs . . .*

☐ *God is helping me to . . .*

*Cast out the scoffer,*
*and contention will leave; yes,*
*strife and reproach will cease.*

PROVERBS 22:10

☐ *Today's challenges and triumphs . . .*
☐ *God is helping me to . . .*

It can be the worst of times and the
best of times at the same time.

☐ *Today's challenges and triumphs . . .*

☐ *God is helping me to . . .*

Crisis does not
make a person.
It simply exposes
them to what they
already are.

☐ *Today's challenges and triumphs . . .*

☐ *God is helping me to . . .*

*The steps of a good man are ordered by the
LORD, and He delights in his way.
Though he fall, he shall not be utterly cast
down; for the LORD upholds him
with His hand.*

PSALM 37:23–24

☐ *Today's challenges and triumphs . . .*

☐ *God is helping me to . . .*

*Wealth gained by dishonesty will be diminished, but he who gathers by labor will increase.*

PROVERBS 13:11

☐ *Today's challenges and triumphs . . .*
☐ *God is helping me to . . .*

*The generous soul will be made rich,
and he who waters will also
be watered himself.*

PROVERBS 11:25

☐ *Today's challenges and triumphs . . .*

☐ *God is helping me to . . .*

*"Be angry, and do not sin": do not
let the sun go down on your wrath,
nor give place to the devil.*

EPHESIANS 4:26–27

☐ *Today's challenges and triumphs . . .*

☐ *God is helping me to . . .*

Acknowledge

someone else's

worth to you.

☐ *Today's challenges and triumphs . . .*

☐ *God is helping me to . . .*

*Let no corrupt word proceed out of your mouth, but what is good
for necessary edification, that it may impart grace to the hearers.
And do not grieve the Holy Spirit of God, by whom you were
sealed for the day of redemption. Let all bitterness, wrath, anger,
clamor, and evil speaking be put away from you, with all malice.
And be kind to one another, tenderhearted, forgiving one
another, even as God in Christ forgave you.*

EPHESIANS 4:29–32

☐ *Today's challenges and triumphs . . .*

☐ *God is helping me to . . .*

"I have coveted no one's silver or gold or
apparel. Yes, you yourselves know that these
hands have provided for my necessities, and for
those who were with me I have shown you in
every way, by laboring like this, that you must
support the weak. And remember the words of
the Lord Jesus, that He said, 'It is more blessed
to give than to receive.'"

ACTS 20: 33-35

# Reflections 4

The apostle Paul reminds us to live our lives with eternity in mind: "Each one's work will become clear; for the Day will declare it, because it will be revealed by fire; and the fire will test each one's work, of what sort it is. If anyone's work which he has built on it endures, he will receive a reward" (1 Corinthians 3:13–14). Accordingly, the apostle John added: "Look to yourselves, that we do not lose those things we worked for, but that we may receive a full reward" (2 John 1:8).

Take time to review the last several pages of this journal. Reflect on all the things you have been discovering about your life. As you've thought about your life in the light of God's Word, what are you learning? What are the most important desires you are expressing to God? What are you discovering that God desires from you? How is He working in your life?

Capture your thoughts on the following pages.

# Reflections